Contents

Highlights
Puzzle Buzz®
Can you find this
buzzing bee?

It is hiding 4 times
on the cover.

S0-BZO-693

Penguin Maze

START

Highlights Puzzle Buzz

FINISH

3

Hidden Pictures

Can you find these 12 items hidden in this camping scene?

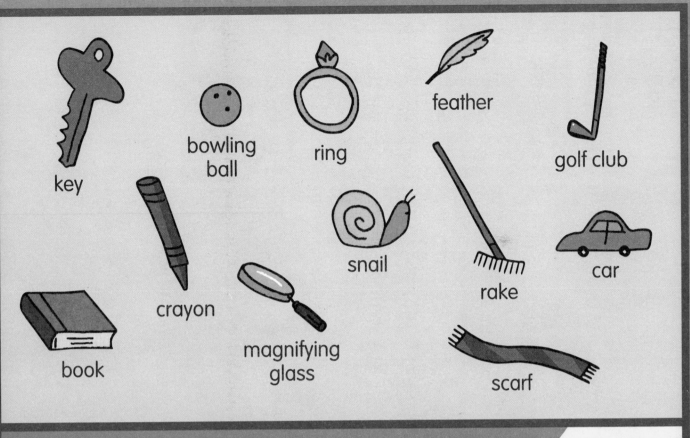

key

bowling ball

ring

feather

golf club

crayon

snail

rake

car

book

magnifying glass

scarf

Dot to Dot

Connect the dots from 1 to 30 to see a useful camping item.

5

Camera Search

There are lots of cameras at this art museum!
Can you find all 13?

Can you find?
- 1 red purse
- 2 pairs of glasses
- 3 books
- 4 hats

ILLUSTRATION BY DONNA CATANESE

Answer on page 30

Double Engine

Ty's class is visiting the fire station. These two pictures are a bit different. Add stickers to this page to make them match.

9

Answer on page 31

Wiggle Pictures

These ways to get around have been twisted and turned.
Can you figure out what each one is?

Answer on page 31

Art Starters

Fill-in Fun Color each space that has a dot to see a big animal.

Color by Number Color this dragonfly.

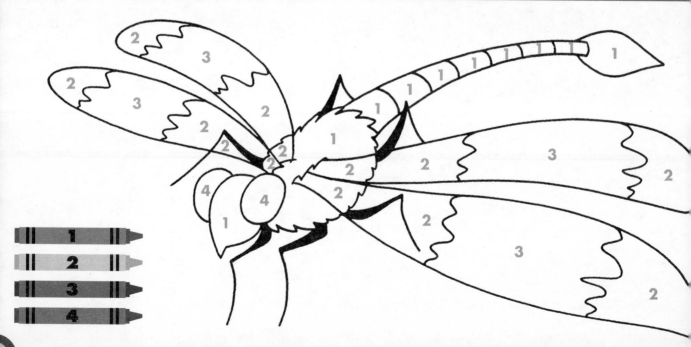

Step by Step Follow the steps to draw a space shuttle.

ILLUSTRATION BY RON ZALME

1.

2.

3.

4.

5.

13

Match Maker

Each of the sunglasses in the picture has another that looks just like it. Find all 10 matching pairs.

Answer on page 31

What's Wrong?®

WHALE

17

ILLUSTRATION BY DAVID COULSON

Try 10

1. What are three words that rhyme with down?

2. Name two planets that start w
the letter M.

3. A stream is usually larger than a river.
○ True   ○ False

4. "Desayuno" is the Spanish word for which meal?
○ breakfast   ○ lunch   ○ dinner

5. Circle the number that is twice as much as 12.

GRRRRRR

24
22
18

6. Name three items you might find in a taco.

7. A doctor for children is called what?
- politician
- pediatrician
- Pinocchio

8. Circle the kite shaped like an oval.

9. Name two countries that start with the letter C.

10. In England, soccer is called "football."
- True   - False

ILLUSTRATION BY KELLY KENNEDY

Hot Dog!

21

Countdown

ILLUSTRATIONS BY RITA LASCARO

Answer on page 32

ILLUSTRATION BY R. MICHAEL PALAN

25

Music Find

The names of 18 music words are hidden in the letters. Some words are across. Others are up and down. We found ORGAN. Can you find the rest?

Word List

BAND
BEAT
DRUM
FLAT
FLUTE
GUITAR
NOTE
~~ORGAN~~
PIANO
SAXOPHONE
SCALE
SHARP
SONG
TROMBONE
TRUMPET
TUBA
TUNE
VERSE

```
S H A R P K Q W J F
A Z G U I T A R Z L
X T U B A R Y J B U
O R G A N U B E A T
P K T R O M B O N E
H Q Z Y F P W K D Y
O S C A L E N O T E
N O Y K A T D R U M
E N Z W T U N E K Z
J G V E R S E Y W Q
```

Highlights **Puzzle Buzz**

Tune Up Draw a picture of an instrument you would like to play.

Answer on page 32

M Is For ?

Can you find a magician, a moose, and a mop? What other things can you find that begin with the letter M?

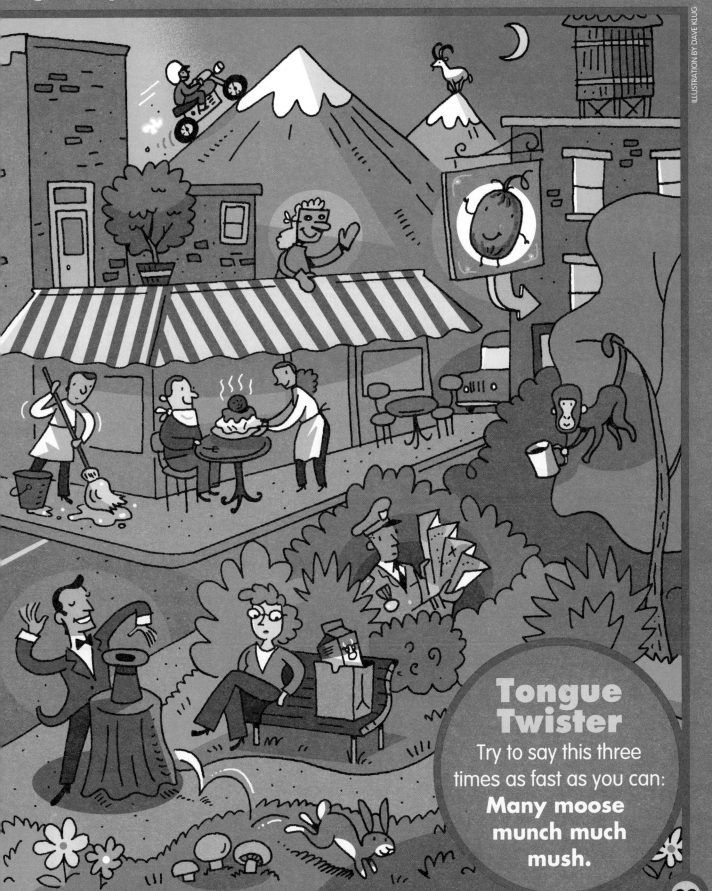

Tongue Twister

Try to say this three times as fast as you can: **Many moose munch much mush.**

29

Answer on page 32

Answers

Cover

2. Penguin Maze

Two of a Kind

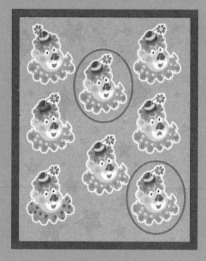

4. Hidden Pictures®

5. Dot to Dot

6. Camera Search

Highlights **Puzzle Buzz**

Answers

8. Double Engine

10. Wiggle Pictures

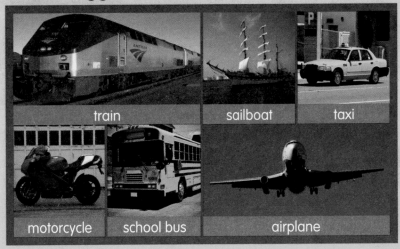

train · sailboat · taxi · motorcycle · school bus · airplane

12. Fill-in Fun

s an elephant!

14. Match Maker

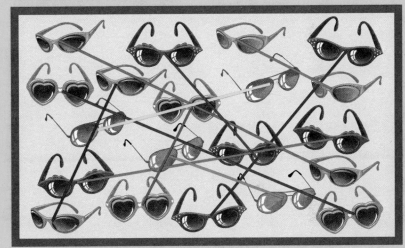

16. What's Wrong?

18. Try 10

1. Clown, crown, frown
   Did you think of others?
2. Mars and Mercury
3. False
4. Breakfast
5. Circle the 24.
6. Lettuce, cheese, and ground beef
7. Pediatrician
8. Circle the kite on the left.
9. Canada and Cuba
10. True

lere are the things we found. You may have found others.

Answers

20. Hot Dog!

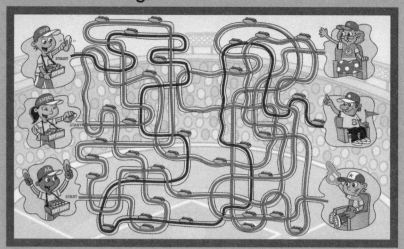

Amber sold the most hot dogs.

22. Countdown

24. Horsing Around

26. Music Find

S	H	A	R	P	K	Q	W	J	F
A	Z	G	U	I	T	A	R	Z	L
X	T	U	B	A	R	Y	J	B	U
O	R	G	A	N	U	B	E	A	T
P	K	T	R	O	M	B	O	N	E
H	Q	Z	Y	F	P	W	K	D	Y
O	S	C	A	L	E	N	O	T	E
N	O	Y	K	A	T	D	R	U	M
E	N	Z	W	T	U	N	E	K	Z
J	G	V	E	R	S	E	Y	W	Q

28. M Is For ?

Here are the M words we found.
You may have found others.

1. map
2. mug
3. milk
4. mask
5. moon
6. medal
7. melon
8. music
9. mirror
10. mouse

11. money
12. magnet
13. monkey
14. minivan
15. mailbox
16. mailman
17. manhole
18. meatball
19. mountain
20. mustache

21. magazine
22. mushroom
23. maple lea
24. motorcycle
25. microscop
26. microphor
27. mountain g

What Is It?

It's a pair of lovebirds!